Never-Ending
BIRDS

BOOKS BY DAVID BAKER

POETRY

Never-Ending Birds (2009)
Treatise on Touch: Selected Poems (2007, UK)
Midwest Eclogue (2005)
Changeable Thunder (2001)
The Truth about Small Towns (1998)
After the Reunion (1994)
Sweet Home, Saturday Night (1991)
Haunts (1985)
Laws of the Land (1981)

CRITICISM

Radiant Lyre: Essays on Lyric Poetry
(edited with Ann Townsend, 2007)
Heresy and the Ideal: On Contemporary Poetry (2000)
Meter in English: A Critical Engagement (edited, 1996)

Never-Ending
BIRDS

❧

POEMS

DAVID BAKER

W. W. NORTON & COMPANY
NEW YORK   LONDON

For information about permission to reproduce selections from this
book, write to Permissions, W. W. Norton & Company, Inc.,
500 Fifth Avenue, New York, NY 10110

For information about special discounts for bulk purchases,
please contact W. W. Norton Special Sales
at specialsales@wwnorton.com or 800-233-4830

Manufacturing by Courier Westford
Book design by Ellen Cipriano
Production manager: Julia Druskin

Library of Congress Cataloging-in-Publication Data

Baker, David, 1954–
Never-ending birds : poems / David Baker. — 1st ed.
p. cm.
ISBN 978-0-393-07018-7
I. Title.
PS3552.A4116N48 2009
811'.54—dc22

2009019638

W. W. Norton & Company, Inc.
500 Fifth Avenue, New York, N.Y. 10110
www.wwnorton.com

W. W. Norton & Company Ltd.
Castle House, 75/76 Wells Street, London W1T 3QT

1 2 3 4 5 6 7 8 9 0

for Katherine Girard Baker

CONTENTS

O N E ✦

Trillium	15
Clean Blade	17
Posthumous Man	18

T W O ✦

The Rumor	25
Horse Madness	28
On Overhearing	32
Ditches for the Poor	34
Before	36
Old Man Throwing a Ball	38
Hungry	39
On Parlance	40
1st My Children	42
Saints' Poppies	45
New World	47
Stranging	48

THREE ❧

Never-Ending Birds	55
Tis a Fayling	56
Middling	59

FOUR ❧

One Willow	63
Hummer	69
Bay	71
Bright Pitch	74
Pseudo Acacia	77
After the Summer Suicides	79
Homecoming	81
Second Tornado	84
Like the Dewclaw	85
Morning and Afternoon	88
Little Orchard	90
Oriole	91

FIVE ❧

The Feast	97
Too Many	100
Resurrection Man	102

NOTES ❧

NOTES	107

ACKNOWLEDGMENTS

These poems first appeared in the following magazines, to whose editors I extend my grateful acknowledgment: *The Alaska Quarterly Review,* "Second Tornado"; *The Atlantic Monthly,* "Hungry"; *The Boston Review,* "The Feast"; *Five Points,* "Middling," "Pseudo Acacia"; *Field,* "1st My Children"; *The Gettysburg Review,* "Stranging," "Trillium"; *The Hopkins Review,* "Oriole"; *The Laurel Review,* "Clean Blade"; *Literary Imagination,* "Before," "Bright Pitch"; *The New England Review,* "Horse Madness," "The Rumor"; *The New Ohio Review,* "New World"; *The New Republic,* "Little Orchard"; *The New Yorker,* "Never-Ending Birds"; *The Paris Review,* "Bay," "Homecoming," "Like the Dewclaw," "Too Many"; *Poetry,* "Saints' Poppies"; *Poetry Northwest,* "After the Summer Suicides"; *Raritan,* "Hummer," "Morning and Afternoon" (part 2); *The Southern Review,* "Posthumous Man"; *The Southwest Review,* "Morning and Afternoon" (part 1); *TriQuarterly,* "Ditches for the Poor," "On Overhearing," "On Parlance," "One Willow," "Tis a Fayling"; *The Virginia Quarterly Review,* "Old Man Throwing a Ball"; *The Yale Review,* "Resurrection Man."

The epigraph is from "Kore" by W. S. Merwin.

I am grateful also to the John Simon Guggenheim Memorial Foundation, the National Endowment for the Arts, the Ohio Arts Council, and Denison University for support and encouragement, and to Jill Bialosky for her faith and guidance.

few are the words for finding

ONE

Trillium

1.
The first year I found it I found it by
accident, working my machete
to make out of the woods a walking path.
Not quite creekside, but in the tree shadow
of the creek, *trilliaceae,* or birthroot,
wake-robin, or any kind of lily
whose petals might wake a robin into
wings, as this does, three-winged if not
creekside, but close, beneath a hedge apple—
itself not an apple. Its blossom is
like a lily, in this case *Trillium*
flexipes (for drooping), as I found
the next year, maroon under three leaves
and swinging there like a bell. The little
brown-red bell blossom was gone the next day.
And the next year: knocked or nosed down by deer.

2.
Picking the flower of trillium can
injure the plant seriously, says my
book. May die or take years to recover.
So I built barricades of small branches,
cages, crossbars, as soon as these new leaves
uncapped, to keep out the deer yet airy
enough to let in some sun, ephemeral
angel wing of blossoms, half as light in
the green long shadow of wild rye grasses.

And the shadowy maroon blossoms hung
for a week—more—browned, peeled, seeded, then dropped.
The next year the drought year. Yet I've found it
again this April, walking the path. Which
is not my path. Not anymore. The deer
have fled, as well, deeper away from us.
And us not us anymore. Obstinate blooms.

Clean Blade

My rawhide gloves, hard machete, I have
my tall boots on, heat like fever crying—you know

where we're heading—deeper in the splayed woods,
ivy vines like forearms wrapped along trunks, helix

of cilia and sinew; cut them in half, else
the hairy stuff will clutch and haul down more,

bramble everywhere, clots in last season's path.
I'm swinging clean, cutting on the bias, pull—

then the heron knows, spray of creek water,
and the mole under my foot, and then my foot

knows, blade slant-cut in the boot. You knew
all along, didn't you? I'm—blood now—last to.

Posthumous Man

I hate the world.
I have come to the edge.

A neighbor's white
bean field in the snow fog.

Three weeks of it
shedding in the warmth

like smoke from fire
lines set against the trees

or the season's
cold boredom with itself.

Mud in the white
field. A hump of gray snow.

Nothing is there.
I hold the dog tight

on his leash. Gray
snow: gray coat, rising now

—scuffed like a bad
rug, scruff-eared—so we watch

nothing rise in
the white bean field and shake

off a night's sleep
and sniff, sniff, peer over

at us. Winter
wrens in a fluff. Rustle

of bramble. He
trots off at precisely

one hundred and
eighty degrees from where

we emerged from
the woods, into the woods . . .

The long married abide in privacy
longer and longer. That's one irony.
After hearing the coyote crying
a week, ten days, maybe more, late at night
through the glassy air, crying like a bird
his song among the billion stars, we saw him
sunning asleep in the neighbor's old field.

And he woke. And saw us. And, unafraid,
loped off. We rise each morning alone from
the shape of our bodies in flannel sheets,
burrow beside burrow, where we dream of
running, bleeding, food, feral sex, each
to his or her own outlandish nightlife.
We walk in the world, we sip our coffee

at a clean glass table, we love our child.
Then come to an edge, where the world
meets the soul, and the soul knows once more
what it holds, such capacity
to inflict harm or injury, easy
as snowfall and fog's long rise back.
It does, it does not, again and again.

I hate the world:
it batters too much the

wings of my self-
will. He's writing to Fanny

a few weeks cold
after the nightingale.

He hears it sing
in lone, full-throated ease.

And knows himself
grown spectre-thin. Even

in sweet incense,
full summer, his sadness is

a bell's bird-call
tolling him *back from thee*

to my sole self!
He'll sail himself, next year—

a man post-
poetry and posthumous,

too numb to feel
the sun over Naples,

to heal his
scavenger lungs. His hands are

white cold. His nails
are ridged, like a field.

He writes, to Brown,
were I in health it would

make me ill. And
means, of course, his heart's lack

—white trees,

        white waves—.

Behind me, winter wind. It whips
the sycamores, whose leaves are large as sheets
of paper, brittle brown or blowing down.
It shakes the blanched-out trunks of beech.
Despite the cold it's humid, a warm
exhaust of fog and breathing of the mud.
Back down the path I cut one summer, down

the ridge and up the drumlin rise beside
the creek, you're reading. Or you're watching
out the window where I vanished with a dog.
I learned when I should leave. There's privacy
you crave, as I do. The irony thereof.
My sheltie wants, growling at his leash, loose.
The coyote would kill him simply—.

So we watch. Long snout. Bone-slender, his high
rear hips. He's a reel of fog unspooling
toward the far, half-shadowed rim of trees.
Uptick of grackles, more wrens—.

                          He's loping.
Now he's running through the field toward the woods.
By the time he is halfway he is gone.

TWO

The Rumor

Come home.
The earth utters
        to the body, and so the body does
        —come home—at last.

Consider thus
the tufts and tail piece,
        hooves cleft from the legs, the legs
        what's left of them where

they dropped con-
centric beneath
        the beech. Consider the beech,
        the lovers' owne

tree, this one, yes,
hearts scored-in
        and someone's, and someone else's, initials
        so swollen

they're unreadable and
more-than-head-
        high-up the trunk.
        Up the trunk—where the body crawled.

Think of that.
A furious, rapt hunger.

We thought it a rumor
when the farmer

called the paper,
when deputies spotted
    something—
    "buff deer or maybe a Dane running

loose in the
corn"—in the feedlot,
    three nights running. Look.
    There is no doubt whatever.

So the body,
even the lover, comes
    down to the earth. But not,
    this time, at first.

The big cat dragged
the corpse up
    the tree—they
    will do that, that's how we know, cats being

climbers
with prey they've killed
    —up, by the bole, the big place,
    to the crotch of the tree, that's what

we call it.
And crouched; ate; shat;

even slept. The claw marks
proceed up the tree. The fleshy

dun bark, blood
stripped brown as
        fox-coat or
        wet sandstone, blood ascending the tree's

evident body. Up
the lovers' tree.
        Then the body fell, at
        least in little pieces,

all around the trunk,
spattered, strewn—
        aureole of deer guts, bitten
        skin, bone. The rest went

on again,
in the body of the beast.
        And so—we hear—the lovers
        do this, too.

Horse Madness

1.
means fury; means heat.
        From *Hippomanes*,
in Ferry's rendering
of Virgil's third georgic:
is slick with froth; is blood-
lipped; is spring-wild.
I see it in your eyes.
The horse is meant,
        like us, for madness.
It must be held in halter

lest it rear or run.
        It must be *scanted of*
leafy foods come
spring, to make it lean,
make it less familiar.
These things Virgil knows.
Yet it may run or rear
or with alarm
        betray your presence,
despite your care.

The eyes go everywhere.
        The eyes are orbital, animal;
they reflect both worlds.
So *Jackanappes-*

on-horsebacke
—weed we hold
as common marigold—
wraps a sun inside
    its petals before
the sun starts down . . .

2.
Their eyes were my clock.
    Thus the oval eyes
of goats and sheep
turn rounder as the day
goes down. Turn round to see,
in thirst, in pain or panic,
what gallops near, whatever
holds itself away, grinding
    in the brooding dust.
What makes Virgil

so compelling, beyond
    the grace of verse, is
farmer knowledge:
thus the shepherd sings
he finds his likeness
in their eyes. His judgment
grows of patience, as
practice grows of prudence,

as goats deserve
no less than sheep deserve . . .

3.
Means burning-in-the-
        marrow; means as-they-
rush-into-the-fire. Meaning
all of us. I look at you
and find—what? Mythology,
song. Thus slaughter begins,
among the bullocks,
when bees are lost
        and must be raised again.
The nose is stopped

(who devised an art
        like this?) and the body
beat until its innards fall.
Then—with marjoram—
a ferment. Then the offal
seeds with bees, and up
they may be gathered.
        Meaning madness
is its own mythology.

The horse begins
        to tremble. The body
shivers; nor whip, nor reins,

nor wide opposing river,
whose rising *can*
bring down mountains,
may hold one back. I see it
in your eyes. Means
    the face I see is not,
my love, my face.

On Overhearing

I can't tell what disaster is can you?
Let's consider the question untethered
from the usual anchors. Fifteen, a-
fire (*are you* still here?), first out of the car,
and still she doesn't run into the house
but whirls, blue wild wind in a tank top.
Her mother is redder by the time she
slams her door, shaking the Sentra, and those
two have at it, girl astraddle the curb,
mom one wing grabbing for something, gnat
in the air now can you?

As the big Canada geese bleat over,
end of August, end of days. One after
another wide tectonic sheet of them
planing the slate sky. So the earth below
slips by, no gasp. I can't tell what is
shifting now the geese sky the earth
keeping my feet can you yet? They flap,
honk—that high automotive—and a feather
in the leaves in the trees (something's happening
somewhere bad I just know it), the leaves
still on the trees but

the color gone, tone of long-washed cloth,
and the little sister is there listening
at the picnic table, brushing their brand-
new rescue dog *Molly the drooler*

Molly mop. The infinite is at hand
only (I read this somewhere, can't recall)
with respect (can you) to the finite. Meaning
look out. As your heart wings toward its own
calling disaster. Then they're done slam slam
going in. It's the little one who does not go in no
                              not for a long while.

Ditches for the Poor

from the French, the middle
    ages—roughly—
as *fosses aux pauvres,*
    denoting common
graves, by which we take to
    mean the practice
of the period by which
    are sewn into
their shrouds the dead,
    the bodies then stacked.
Language is, in itself,

    already
skepticism, writes Levinas.
    A fissure
opens. An opportunity
    for, what,
clarity? Closure, perhaps,
    through which these
instances of proximity
    may be—.
When the graves became
    crowded—there,

imagine the ninety lumps,
    the layers
of dirt dividing strata
    of bodies,

the several-yards-by-
        several-yards hole
having been filled—the church-
        keeps redug
the ditch, disinterred
        the nameless in
decay to install the newer

        dead. Old bones
to the charnel hall. There is
        no narrative
to such anguish, as from
        the corpse no odor.
As from a gathering loss
        mere ennui.
Think of the others
        —the grieving living—
waiting, with their needles,
        to stitch anew.

Before

Broken parts
    bring us back to
    each other. From

where? How
    does such shatter
    (does it?) knit?

And for when? Into
    what form, knit; or for
    how long a

durance will
    repair so stay?
    I ask because,

like slow out-
    flow of a pond I once held
    close—swept out, of its

Styrofoam, water-
    meal, netted dead-
    nettle; fished there; stocked

there, repaired (did I say?)—
    once wild new water
    shoves free and

finds a running ditch,
　　　　it will be swept
　　　　altogether beyond

that other body, not
　　　　its own.
　　　　That body (do

you hear?) having
　　　　been broken by
　　　　this water,

which found it
　　　　otherwise, and first (please),
　　　　as it was. Before you——.

Old Man Throwing a Ball

He is tight at first, stiff, stands there atilt
tossing the green fluff tennis ball down
the side alley, but soon he's limber,
he's letting it fly and the black Lab

lopes back each time. These are the true lovers,
this dog, this man, and when the dog stops
to pee, the old guy hurries him back, then
hurls the ball farther away. Now his mother

dodders out, she's old as the sky, wheeling
her green tank with its sweet vein, breath.
She tips down the path he's made for her,
grass rippling but trim, soft underfoot,

to survey the yard, every inch of it
in fine blossom, set-stone, pruned miniature,
split rails docked along the front walk,
antique watering cans down-spread—up

huffs the dog again with his mouthy ball—
so flowers seem to spill out, red geraniums,
grand blue asters, and something I have
no name for, wild elsewhere in our world

but here a thing to tend. To call for, and it comes.

Hungry

This time the jay, fat as a boot, bluer
than sky gone blue now that the rain has
finished with us for a while, this loud jay
at the neck of the black walnut keeps cawing
I want, I want—but can't finish his clause.
Hard runoff has spread the driveway with seeds,
green talcum, the sex of things, packed
like plaster against shutters and tool boxes,
sides of the barn, while the force of water
pouring down from the stopped-up gullet
of gutter has drilled holes deep in the mud.
Yet the world of the neighborhood is still just
the world. So much, so much. Like the bulldog
next door, choking itself on a chain
to guard the yard of the one who starves it.

On Parlance

He was packed with gear,
    and in the parlance
of the ever ready, he was
good to go, *thumbs up.*
He was halfway out
the squad before it stopped.
    His partner, equally
can-do and equipped,
having left the truck
at idle, dogged his heels
across the neighbors' porch
    and slammed the screen.
There we were at windows,

worrying who'd died
    or taken ill, fallen through
the night. Red lights
raced the yard, the yard
next door, to ours,
to trace the artery
    of road and rural heart
—this one's box farmhouse,
this one's smoke tree manor—
the countryside less
neighborhood than scattered
    arclights, cankered
barns, and gutless cars.

What could it mean our
        neighbors' yard was junk,
heady weeds and broken
muddy glass, three dogs
tethered by day like
charms against civility—yet
        their garden a perfection:
peas on strings, raised beds
of corn, cutting flowers
strictly rowed by color,
height. You could see their
        working as a kind of play.
I haven't mentioned the crisis

that kept us up at night.
        When the driver came out,
slow steps, and stowed
their gear, the animal
growl of the diesel idling, we
couldn't tell what happened.
        Then *the first one in,*
the last one out, who
turned and slowly waved
into the neighborhood,
the night. What did it mean?
        It could mean all was well.
It could mean good-bye.

1st My Children

1.

whom I do love is
Polly Collins's gift drawing in what looks like
seam work but is pencil underneath ink
and watercolor applied to paper.
The background of her art is cloud, summer—
six trees, spreading, inside boxes. Symmetry's
her devotional: such being the shape
         of artistry held in a hand.

2.

1854—
June. Her numbered cursive monostich tells,
above her tree grid, the latest vision,
as, *5th When upon Earth my care was great*
Afflictions oft I felt. One blazing tree
spread below, as by an angel, "as dis-
tinctly as I ever saw a natural
         tree"—as, *6th When many times*

3.

my frame was shook, This
gave me strength for to perform My Duty . . .
below which, the tree aflame; one tree that
holds out, eight arms full, its fruit, its safe nest;
or this, her largest tree, whose tongues are blooms.
But now my girl calls from her room.

She's hungry, she's bored. She wants a little
         attention. So I set the book

4.

aside to listen . . .
are you reading that tree thing again? As,
*Though dragon like in manmade form, Some rage
to and fro.* As I have raised my voice. Or
raised my hand. Or, slower fury, closed
myself off with books and witless chores.
She's with me three days out of seven.
         The flowers have ears: Polly shapes

5.

her delicate panes
so the picture's a peaceful house—and full
flat leaves uprisen on pointillist bark.
Once I threw a toy across the room. Once
again I ask my child's forgiveness,
who's singing with her friend SpongeBob.
Now a bright cardinal flicks to the fringe bloom
         and starts to whet, like a blade, his

6.

hooked beak. Scatter of
notes—our subsong—beneath the lavender-
lit froth of flowers. I told her a story

once. Once a little girl lived in a nice
white house, a hundred times and more those nights
I raged to stay in my head. Tomorrow
off she goes. Hold my hand. Before I'm through
this story we could be asleep.

Saints' Poppies

Somewhere they are weeds beside the long road
—lord of mishandling, lord unbefitting—.

They are red ruined by rainwater or
the rust of a rebar tossed in disuse.

Nightingales name them across the chasm.
But not this one, who crooks her swollen finger

to stroke them,
                to dowse them with a little drink . . .

      Somewhere they are weeds beside a long road
so potted by wagon wheels it's ruined,

almost, for walkers pulling toward market.
Now she's lined her pocket with their clippings

and would fill another, had she another.
Which saints? She won't say. It's her name for them

in lieu of their names. She unpeels a few
petals, pale as crepe—leaves in her good book—.

My book calls them bare root, spice, *Papaver
orientale Turkenlouis,* or meadow

variety red corn-poppy. They are
bred for ornament, oils, opium, food.

Somewhere—not here—they are weeds to curse
beside steep houses, along stacked stone walls,

under the arthritis of olive trees.
And no one, not for ages, shall bless them.

New World

—Yellow gingkos, awash on the sidewalks.
But we can't have them. Blue sky like a just-
thrown vase. Bright plain blue side still glowing.
Autumn air. Warm as a bath. We can't say so.
We did not see them the horses nuzzle
in the field, in the muddy pen, in the big acres
hidden by trees in the middle of the financial city,
nor whisper through a night in a booth. In
a room. In no hurry atop sheets of many gone loves.
This was not us, nor will be, nor ever will I
forget you when the broken histories are told.
Expenditure and loss. Collateral and gift.
. . . *no where shall Wee Be known.* How
many leaves. How much wind in the new world—.

Stranging

Of tribulation they write little. Less
of pain. There are words for the strange fowl,
humped as boles on the raw branches, black-capt
and gold fincht, and for the wild songs therefrom.
There are words for trees that shelter these birds—
low laurels, others that are called liquid-
ambars, cedars, savins and evergreen oaks—
but these trees. But these birds. De Vaca said

he viewed the New World with old eyes. Some things
so strange he recounted them, if at all, as
piecemeal, as figments or genera, or
got the species wrong. 1528.
The trees are simply trees he's guessing at.
And black turkeys scuttling through the broom-brush.
And alligators he'd have watched, roiling
the rich cypress swamps—no words at all.

Where we walked I see
a sharp-shinned hawk, flared

tail crossed with feathers,
dip and flee. And see

tulip poplars in
the dreadful breeze shed

a mass of seeds on-
-the-wing—samara,

one book says—to deaden
the woods' flooring.

Perch shiners plumb, still
alive, the cold creek.

A hard early winter.
All I have are words.

Where we walked in thick
woods (two kingfishers,

"rarely found away
from the water," blow

off the pond, up, to
the hills) now I go

with my accuracy
and old sorrow.

Taylor has his word for wondering, thus
stranging. He sings in a voice like a crow

sometimes, sometimes like a locust, clagd, skied.
Pastor doctor father, feral of words,
he passed a life alone among the rest
to wring his language (now writh the Divells-
bit with a Blow) out of the unfit. Now
presst his pestle for a dire patient.

1680. And saw birds as Authour's
Allegory: himself on this bough not long.
Th'Infernall Foe shot out a Shaft from Hell,
a Fiery Dark Pild with Sins poison strong:
That struck my heart. As I feel, kneeling here.
Snowcrust in the cups of seed husks. Brutal
thistle, crown-of-thorns. Arctium, the book
says. Heart-shaped leaf. Poisonous in legend.

And when a lark flies
up, I know its name:

E. alpestris, no
other lark being

native to this world.
Ground nester, like me,

whose least and common
singing (says the book)

floats high-pitched, lisping
or tinkling, and weak.

To see each thing clear
is still not to see

a thing apart from
words or our wild need.

Your absence a light
by which the snow shines:

wind that hefts the wings
of what flies away—.

De Vaca feared the trees were poisonous.
Thus the Susolas yielded—gifts—the hearts
of six hundred deer. In turn he cured one
lost man, "who was dead, whose house was undone."
Modorra, says the book, illness whose
victim grows unconscious, as to death. Thus
baskets of crushed prickly pears. Much weeping.
Then the one who had been dead is risen.

I have these disconcerting facts. Ivy
like wretched legs around the trunk it chokes
holds up the tree. A wood teal flies, before

we know it's there. Of tribulation, of
hurt, of yearning, they write little—let
the world stand for what they know. Of yearning.
I have you in my hands and then you're gone.
White swan. White shadow crossing the black pond.

THREE

Never-Ending Birds

That's us pointing to the clouds. Those are clouds
of birds, now we see, one whole cloud of birds.

There we are pointing out the car windows.
October. Gray-blue-white olio of birds.

Never-ending birds, you called the first time—
years we say it, the three of us, any

two of us, one of those just endearments.
Apt clarities. Kiss on the lips of hope.

I have another house. Now you have two.
That's us pointing with our delible whorls

into the faraway, the trueborn blue-
white unfeathering cloud of another year.

Another sheet of their never ending.
There's your mother wetting back your wild curl.

I'm your father. That's us three, pointing up.
Dear girl. They will not—it's we who do—end.

Tis a Fayling

Thus, my guilt; of my shame, corresponding;
    and anguish, like blood on an egg, I have
nothing more to say, for I am stretched up
    bare in a clover field under many
mad stars. I am unfit wholly in the
    just eyes of the lord of stars, I am not
(listen, you can hear this fayling sunder
    the smeared trees) with my breath, nor of it; or
I am in a white bed not my own; or
    my own. Liquid not dew bruising my face.
I can lick it in my lip corner. (Tis
    a fayling of his expectation). As,
who can endure to have their love despised?
    Among men who shall know? But of my part
I shall no more speak, unless I make worse
    this deficiency. From his fearful
poetry, all tending to depress
    the Creator, thus his warning (which
I do not heed) to prepare them for
    Necessity, End, and Usefulness of
Afflictions. 1669. For sure his
    Power shines forth in our Infirmity.
How prepare? Even Reverend Wigglesworth,
    "enduring the most dreary, unproductive,
lonely period of his life," becomes
    living proof of the necessity
of afflictions. Thus Bunker his associate
    expires; thus daughter Mercy so departs;

his Esther dies "though the exact date is
        unknown"; and his voice lifts up as never
stronger in fierce alarm. What means this
        Paradox? Afflictions are like Ballast
i'th' Bottom of a Ship, yet every
        puff would quickly set us over, and sink
us in the Ocean Sea no more for to
        Recover. I have nothing more to say
yet am my body's own, of evidence.
        Of my shame (see the towers how they once
again evaporate), I carry (see men
        flying, as if swallows wing-shot) (a boy
in Baghdad coddling his mother's eye in
        his palm) blood on the egg (now of Black Ops
in a narrow valley, beneath the swept
        mountains of Caracas). I carry my
lover's breath as a precious stone. And are
        these (yes they are) my fayling? Of my part
I have no more words, for my breath is not
        with me, she is with me, constellation
of winged things beneath the barnlight breathes
        over our skin like a savored thing.
It is a savored thing. And yet I find
        a heart, he moans, so dead, and I have found
prevailing this week such a Spirit of
        whoardoms and departure, I am afraid
of my owne Vile Heart that I shall one day
        fall. Thus fall. "After twenty years of

'widoehood' and almost constant distress,

    Wigglesworth scandalizes——," and Mather must
renounce them both, Wigglesworth his former

    tutor, and she "your servant mayd of obscure
parentage, & of no church . . . I question

    whether the like hath bin known in the Christ-
ian world." (Thus my mouth her tongue the waters

    ripe and rippling through our body of the
world.) Everywhere this breathing skin resounds.

    So I may not speak? Then Lord I must sing.

Middling

1.

Of the fringe—neither edge nor periphery
but green in the darker green middle height
of the tree. Of the tassel, one kind, which
blooms. Of its pale green-white tiny flowers
produced in feathery panicles, each
a corolla made of four slender lobes
which the little brown birds perturb, as though
bathing in the bloom. And, in fall, redbirds
scatter these seeds to the ground—.

2.

The body is more light than not. And swift
into flight if need be or the heart says.
You let my hand go in the pale fall air.
Chionanthus virginicus, or white
fringe tree, old-man's-beard, or Grancy's gray.
The name is less strange than the fringe. You let
my hand go to go. Each drupe being the fruit
of the fringe and holding a single seed,
which the birds love to scatter to the ground.

3.

We were wrong about the thing—great wooden
farm machine shaped like a piano
with all its player parts, only bigger,
or a casket, only bigger. Polished
a thousand times and more simply by use.

The raw whole husks go in, he showed us how,
to sift chaff from the wheat heart of the grain—
the soft seed center which is ground further
as flour. But the middling shakes to its ground-

4.
level bin, too, as food, if not for us:
filler for the hogs, tillage for the fields.
As the tree is filled with light, humming, wings—.
And these strange green pale fringes like lamplight
in the middle of dusk, whose leaf persistence
is the last difference between
deciduous fringe and evergreen species
known the world away. You let my hand go.
And the birds scatter the seeds to the ground.

FOUR

One Willow

Willow delights
in a moist and wet soil
        —here being *Salix babylonica*—
        so notes Edward Stone. Then adds

(to the Royal
Society): *where ague*
        chiefly abounds.
        Consider the genius of

the doctrine. *When*
find ye a thing
        seek
        there its cure. Or,

localize the lore.
Across the
        bramble floodplain, ivy thickens
        with a talc of poisons

and beside it—root unto root—the pale gem
jewelweed,
        taller, many-round-pronged ovate leaf
        and sallow bloom, so

we've learned
to snap the stalk, smear a drop

of sap to
cool and clear

an ivy bite.
Reverend Stone,
            faith being a genus of need,
            put his mouth to the thing—

Crack willow, its name. The ice broke
the top branches down until it was stripped,
a glassine mass of shards shining fire
in morning's hard light. Whip willow
—a thing being its name—or torch to light
the way, to bury the dead by the path.
One willow, our willow, grew by the pond.
Grew shaggy; grew down. With leaves
in "finely toothed margins," the book said,
"and furnished with the two small leaf-like
appendages, known as 'stipules,' at their bases."
Its bracts fringed with hair. Its leaves "convolute—
i.e. rolled together in the bud, like
a scroll of paper," tapered to points, fine-
serrated, gray bloom at the underside . . .

—and tasted there of quinine,
bitter remedy

for malaria. Dried
for three months in a baking oven

a pound of
willow bark. Applied this
        to fifty more—faith being antidote
        to suffering, in this case

rheumatism—to which
each responded
        with excellent result.
        Thus salicylates, for a century

following, yield an
acid analgesic
        for healing (headache, heartache, shredded
        muscle, sore or torn tendon . . .);

and yield for
Bayer Pharmaceutical, in 1899,
        a formula for "the most popular
        drug in the world."

Find ye what ye need
among its other.
        Other being, by the doctrine of signatures
        set forth by Philippus Theophrastus

Aureolus Bom-
bastus von Hohenheim—a.k.a.

Paracelsus—c. 1530,
nature's way of making meaning, counterpoint, and

remedy to each poison, each disease,
each bodily discomfiture. Nature
being God's provident gift of usage.
Thus lungwort, to cure pulmonary stains;
thus gravelwort (urinary stones) and
bloodroot for vomiting; maidenhair fern
to mend baldness. Thus shaking palsy
is overcome by poplar (as quaking
aspen) leaves; and lily of the valley,
writes William Cole, *cureth apoplexy*
by Signature; for as that disease is
caused by the dropping of humours into
the principal ventricles of the brain:
so the flowers of this Lily hanging
on the plants as if they were drops, are of

wonderful use herein.
—Switch willow, our
        tree, or broom, for the wealth of downfall after
        wind, the implements we might make.

But this time: sleet,
great snow, then

gale, from which
our willow shattered downward, ice-

toppled, explosive
over deep drifts, and shone
        for days in the sun to follow.
        One willow.

For our gathering, as
leaves to burn,
        limbs
        to sweep; as holding hands

with our child, to sing there
to a cat buried
        with his ball, a little food,
        and a willow switch to dig his way out;

as in to amass, under-
stand, stand
        be-
        neath, fold, as

hands, as in harvest,
as a storm will
        gather, or army will, or something wholly
        unforeseen but, now, in-

evitably broken on the white ground
around us and nothing to do but grieve.
Thus weeping, for the shape of its branches,
the shed leaf, a shudder of things in wind.
Weeping, as the story of our willow,
and something else that grew, root unto root,
beside us, beneath, within, instead.
Suffering being antidote—.
Thus petal of iris, *a bruise polstice*;
and Saint-John's-wort, writes John Gerard, *with oile
the color of blood, remedie for deep wounds.*
Once a willow grew beside a fine pond.
Two shadows lived in its shadow. And raised
a child. And watched a ruining storm, which
—we hardly believed our eyes—was a sign
of the life one comes to find as one's own.

Hummer

The greater the lesser, the cars bulked up
and armored for the exurban, panic-
room set, for whom a wide wheelbase
is a military presence on the highway,
superior—if insecure—in its security.
A strip of highway, and then they blow by.
And the long blast aftereffect, like the pitch
that flies by the same name, the brush-back
warning shot of a little *chin music,* what
the veterans call from the dugout.
All you see is a wing then feel the whir.

They're out there now, the lesser the faster,
each fury-borne blur with a ruby ribbon
at the throat of the meanest thing
on wings, diving to suckle at sugar-
water tubes we dangle from our pin oaks,
stealing sips from coral bells or the pink
hoods and human poisons of a foxglove.
We love to watch them. Though watch, precisely,
isn't right. They shoot, dart, flipper away
at astonishing rates—seventy-five wing-
and twelve heartbeats per second, unless

courting, during which the tenuous wing-
member vibrates two hundred times a tick.
All we catch is a pencil-line fading-
in-water escape. Or the rare instance

of a landing, when one whirs to a pine bough
—blue finger, with a beak—then back, back
to bombing each other, bumping windows.
What drives them if not hunger's hundred shapes,
hatred, thirst, mania, survival, force of habit?
Each is greater than the last, according to
the laws of compensation and revenge.

Bay

Heat shirrs the water
where it's spilled—*have to
get him in
    just the right spot,*

*it's
quick, he'll go
heavy when his back hits
    the grass*—trough like a silver sleeve

at the barn side.
Now my neighbor flicks (it's
thick as a Coke
    bottle) his hypo. Says

now and the colt
tips over,
forgets those slender knees.
    And now he swabs a spot—

have to hurry—clippers
the musky hide down
to the skin
    brown as a grocery sack and

ties his
hind leg, then the other.

It's my job to pull the risen one, spread
    up, woody mirage in the mud

across the pen,
rope behind my neck,
arm eagled out
    along the running guywire, colt's

hoof high in the air.
Now my friend's got his
vicious tool more
    like a sharp sickle or meat hook than a

surgical device,
but really
that's what it is, silver hook
    to slit

the tough skin and
tease out the testicles,
so he does, hand
    inside, snip snip, tossing the first small

red wad
for the dog—but *goddamn* is
what he says, ooze now, some flesh-
    bubble, and the anesthesia

already easing off—
close him up

before it's all leaked out—undevel-
   oped wall and herniating guts where the hand is still

half in, *can't do this* . . .
But the colt
is bobbing his neck, leg
   pulled harder along my neck rope, a little shit

running from his tail:
what I meant
to say is
   —it happens so fast—I grabbed his

neck, fingers in his mane
as he softened, first, to fall,
and that's
   when I thought of us, dancing

in the dining room,
hands in each other's
clothes and the woody bay-plant's
   saucer overfull, and one

leaf snapped—that's it, that scent—.

Bright Pitch

A few survive, black-
shellacked and
     bannered with ads
     (as, *Chew Mail Pouch
Tobacco*), but the un-
subsidized implode—

faint shadows
of plank rot, straw
     mulch, ghost hardware
     and tractor car-
casses wrecked and ribbed
as things Cretaceous.

Wood barns are,
floating the vast
     fields of Ohio, rarer
     than specks of matter
in the blown heavens.
As: one barn =

10^{-28}
square meters:
     a single nu-
     clear particle in
cross section.
The term being

code at the Manhattan
Project (*couldn't*
    hit the side
    of—) for the rarity
of finding such universe
stuff. The proximate

figure: one gram
per 1,000 earth-
    volumes. But (more
    from our sponsors)
why do we want
to blow to bits

every last speck of things?
—whatever's ex-
    pendable, explodable,
    of no more
good than wood sides
now that sheet-

metal pole barns
have rendered them
    obsolete: fallible.
    So fall they do.
When bomb makers
hit the right

proportions of
uranium to a-
     mass, fabricating
     the first
nuclear blast,
did they know

where such elegant de-
signing would
     lead? As today,
     for instance:
four below, snow
blistering down

Madison Avenue. Here's
a shop window big as (of
     course) a barn door.
     Your Favorite White
Fur Boots! Mittens
in Cashmere!

The door's blocked
open. Hot air blooms
     over the walk, and
     the season's bright pitch:
Come In   Let Us   (toy
poodle, half-nude mannequin)

Blow You Away!

Pseudo Acacia

1.

for false thorned—for though it bears thorns, these do
not cover each whole tree; not black-hooked, paired,
rigid, nor as of weapons. Nor as plague,
on delicate wings, though its name sounds
of real alarm. The black locust is
deeply furrowed, tinged with red, branchlets
coated at first with white silvery down.
Then prickles develop from stipules, short,
sharp, dilated at the base, as leaves grow
odd-pinnate, parallel, and compound. None
of this we saw, speeding, from the highway.

2.

Each whole treetop shimmers, as in a cloud.
Pale white, white-green, pendulate from the limbs,
its flowers color a running woods in
a color of clouds. And like clouds, born in
loose cream-white drooping racemes, locust
blossoms are nectar-bearing and -lipped, sweet.
We did not know what we saw, nor its name.
We were running somewhere to find some peace.
The road cut the hills, close-rock-cropped, veined, then
again we'd open into flat land—locust
trees flaring among the fir and oak woods.

3.

By peace I mean we didn't know ourselves,
only that we hungered, only hoped some
other place would heal us, or bring us ease,
at least in name. Famous is the locust
for hardness, high heat in fire, for fencing—
famous in ships, to knock down cannonballs
at its fiercesome sides. Only later
did we read what we'd seen floating
in the woods. When we arrived, I don't
know where, the wind turned white with petals.
Then the air filled with the real scent of honey.

After the Summer Suicides

One is asleep in the saddle and one is half asleep,
slumping, half conscious in the miles-high air.

It's so cold a breath is a bite of white water.
One or two have drifted off the path—the rest of you

are trying not to look down. Or you look down
into the glacial green bowl, yawning below.

Your legs want to float out of the stirrups.
It's easier to look down than look down the side

of the mountain, which is to look over nothing
a mile or more across the ridge cutting away rising.

You are scanning the sky for a high hawk calling
—pull the horses up to see—and it's a herd of elk

on the ridge like a flock, a field of wild laurels,
the far, seagull cry of the calves. Now the herd

rolls off in waves, the young staggering across
the stone face where the cows nuzzle them along,

the bulls lagging, looking back. You hear them
calling long after they are gone. The rest of the ride

you feel blessed by the grass, shivering white-
trunked aspens you come down to, cold white streams

you cross and recross, letting the horses
dip their noses in and drink and huff, down

from the place where the water must choose,
west to the ocean, or east, so far, so slow, to the sea.

Homecoming

Black coffee for Amanda,
sipping the white steam—Jessica says
    we have to
    hurry or the good dresses

will be gone: no
homecoming for you. She's got a
    sticky bun, cinnamon,
    enough caramel icing for a bundt cake,

grape juice, and so
does Sarah,
    who's doing social studies
    last minute in loopy green ink

in her Beyoncé
ring binder. Big girls.
    They're fourteen,
    they're freshwomen, and with my Kate meet

each Wednesday, at
8, at the Daily Grind, late-
    arrival day at high school.
    I'm the dad. My task is to load them at 8:50

back into my truck,
windows down, music up,

and drop them off by 9.
Natalie's got her field hockey uniform on already,

stretchy blue knee socks, plaid
skirt, white Under Armour (shorts),
insignia duffel (big as a body bag) with
her stick, more

pads, water bottle, school-color
scrunchies, who knows . . .
The other man in the shop's
reading a tabloid. *Why Doesn't the World*

Love the U.S.? The girls
know. We're stupid, we
start wars, we have too much
stuff, and then they're off on the Odyssey

—the real one—for
English reports. Each
girl's got five minutes
and a tale to tell: homecoming (again)

and the hero's loyal
hound; the sirens
(they're like the Veela
in Harry Potter—*Half-Blood Prince?* no no no,

says Katie: *Goblet of Fire*—
only nicer. They're *so* not

nice, Morgan whiffs).
But what about the loom? Ohmygod (Sarah),

why does Penelope
keep knitting if
        he's not coming home? It's
        freaky. Why

untie all that stuff? *Honey.*
He comes home. Sarah:
        [sigh]. By now I don't know, I just
        don't know, girls. Then

another mom walks by and gives me that look
—I'm hot, I'm
        the dad—.
        Then Hollis says, Gee

Morgan's moody today. Kiss kiss. *Thus they sette sail.*

Second Tornado

This time the porch seems to pitch to the side.
Or is everything else shoved that way? Blown
yellow, yellow-green, leaf chaff in big sheets
flying across the porch hard from the side.
What you hear about the train isn't true.
Yet there are passengers riding the rails
of the wind, larks awing, a wild meadow
variety but more like confetti

than birds, and pages of evening news
in a real hurry. And the gray-green sky
isn't true, unless the flailing hung ferns
like electrocuted dolls are enough
in the sky to count. Now the squad's
streaming the block, a lookout for downed lines.
And now the banging of the porch eaves is
inside the eaves. Now the harder rain—

the first was Kansas, devil-in-the-heat,
yet it lifted shingles off a flat house
and tore the tar paper, toys in the yard,
then the roof as we watched from the ball field.
She was elsewhere, nobody to me then,
unmet for decades coming on. O
wind. O wild love. Whirl me in the sky
sideways to her now and toss me down.

Like the Dewclaw

1.

The trees, the ones
she loves,
     are desperate—
      healthy vines have

twined to clamber up
their trunks.
      Grape climbers in the canopy.
      Understory of branches

dripping bark but dry as paper-char.
Red squirrels run
     the tops of
     trees, never touching earth.

2.

The gods are comic,
who will
     not perish.
     My love takes pictures of

each wilding mass
she finds: pays
     no mind to clarity but tangle gives her
     mind the chaos-close-to-comfort

that she craves:
her word.

      What are feelings for?
      Above the green good grass

3.
she props a whirl of
twigs and stems until it's spinning into haze.
      Snap. Ten thousand tendrils
      grabbing hair-

fine at the poplar's trunk.
Snap.
      When we love
      we are so swept:

whose trouble
the gods decreed as tragedy.
      We see the infinite
      only once,

4.
thorn of bramble
like the dewclaw of a dog,
      vestigal thumb
      that serves no further use.

When we love
we never touch the ground

but, as in a fleet run,
brush the

leaning grass—

all around, the twisting rough chaotic thing we crave.

Morning and Afternoon

1.

He's alone in the lane meant for bikers
and power walkers, whose stride looks like they're
punching something in the air. Slow spinning,
right shoulder aimed down to the center
of the city's gravity, he's sort of
singing—something about birds, water, wading—.
Now a service truck makes its turn at the curb,
so he knocks the fender, peers in, goes
back dancing to his cart with its books and
cups, his corduroy coat of plastic arms.
Rain in the night has pooled the low places—
he toes at one, an oily shimmering,
then shakes his cuff but keeps spinning
as passersby maintain their distances. Not
this girl, hopping to him in her yellow
slicker. She stops to consider. Now her mother
pulls her back in line in the line of walkers
checking their messages, texting, talking
to people on high floors in other cities
above dancers whirling down slowly
like water only to surface one morning
somewhere else in a city of great dreams.

2.

A minute, no more,
        and it's over—
his *Screw you*

buckles into fighting
and a blade cuts his neck
        to the bone.
So he's strapped
        to the gurney, screaming,
good hand flailing,
        while the EMTs
squelch the blood
        and a cop keeps
one side of the street
        away from the other.
Then someone scrubs
        the mess off the curb.
Then the fire in
        the trashed car goes out.
You can hear last week's
        rain still gurgling
along the culverts
        beneath the street.
And for the longest while
        nothing else
happens—birds, shoppers,
        a faint breeze—
a few red lights clenching,
        unclenching . . .

Little Orchard

How many trees—miniature at that—
before we call it an orchard. How much
pleasure bobs there, for how many songbirds.
Something so big in the little fruit trees.
Yet one peck and they spoil the juvenile fruit.
And the deer lean their whole earthly weight
to the mesh fencing, scraping the mild
derma of trunks down to the infant bone.
And beetles drink the last precious sap
as we drink the sap of what's left, even
after it's dry. And fly away, separate,
each to a high separate limb. Crisp leaves.
And the green pears shrivel hard as nuts.
And something strips the sour cherry overnight.
Fruit for the beast. Not a leaf left for love.

Oriole

—Of such moment, the paper has noted
its appearance in the park, *icterus,*
of the family *Icteridae,* rare
this far east but not to be confused with
Oriolidae, the Old World species,
though they are "strikingly similar," if
superficially, in size, behavior,
diet, such masks and dry chatter, such low
chucks, such orange-over-black, and thin *weenk,*
their wingspan of equal length in adults.
The birders are mad with it, calling

with catalogue whistles and suited up
for long mornings in the wilds. Tape buffs
want to pinpoint the trill in the city's
noisy flights—its chaos and jeers, siren
songs of tragedies, or about-to-be—.
Now someone spots the dun-and-dust female.
Now someone points to a nest sagging in
a plane tree; someone climbs. It's just a piece
of pantyhose filled out with leaves.
So many hopefuls, looking to the clouds
or cloudy textures of buildings and vines.

I watched for the oriole but didn't
see it but the sun hadn't hit that spot.
I bet we will see it come spring or now
if we're there in the sun. Your e-mail on

a jaundiced Sunday. Does it help to know
they're drawn to insects, nectar, cut citrus?
That *icterus* is Greek for yellow, one
association of which means illness?
It's a nice place for a little bird. Plus
there's an enormous old, I think, elm there.
I moved the orchids to the window ledge

to catch the sun. Remember the purple
one? It's going to bloom again! Can hardly
wait to see you Saturday. "Oriole"
is first recorded (in the Latin form
oriolus) by Albertus Magnus
in 1250. The last I saw was low
and lone, on a lightning-blasted beech limb,
blazing like the flag of its nation. This
was a small stand of old-age trees, the last
among two hundred acres cut for growth
beside the soybean fields behind my house.

By growth, I mean exurban housing lots.
The farmer's a millionaire now. I look
for you in faces in the city crowds.
I listen in the nightmare dark—,
but my madness is small compared to
so many others' grief and hunger,
to so much want. *Convergent evolution,*
"whereby organisms not related
independently evolve the same traits

in adapting to similar environs."
Right now a really beautiful white one

is blooming on long low spears. In the park
the reporter finds no bird. He decides
nature isn't necessarily elsewhere.
It's the person holding binoculars,
as much as the bird in the tree. New World
Orioles are known to migrate great
distances. They nest in thickened foliage,
by low riversides. White wing bars, variable
black on top—do you think me fond?—
they prefer to be hidden, singing
variably, too, fast jumbles, whistles,

chopped warbles, then a run of melody.
Long the days and nights for weeks without you,
so we send these messages. Are you happy?
Do you know that coltsfoot helps with asthma?
You should write about the city, you should
write a positive thing. Right now making
decaf coffee. I'm ready for a walk.
Look out your window first. See the movement
in the park, in the commerce, on the streets.
The loud mad wilderness of so many
and so much. I am out there. Wave your hand—.

FIVE

The Feast

The moon tonight is
the cup of a
      scar. I hate the moon.
      I hate—more—that scar. My love waited

one day, then half
the next. One
      cyst drained of fluid that looked,
      she said, like icing for

a cake. *Red-*
laced, she said, *gold,*
      tan, thick, rich. Kind of
      beautiful.

One cyst
was not a cyst. One
      —small one, hard, its edges jagged—
      like a snow ball.

This one scared
the house on-
      cologist into
      lab work: stat.

Once the snow melts the birds
will be back.

Once
many men were masked

in front of their
families. Were gunned down
        to shallow graves, together, there.
        Basra. Kaechon. East

St. Louis, Illinois. Nowhere
we don't know about
        and nothing yet is done.
        This is what we watch while

we wait.
Twelve little cysts
        of snow in the red-
        bud. I watched each one, having

counted, once more, and then one
more time, as
        the news reports reported
        and the cold early

northern wind shook
out there the bare, still-budded small
        bush. Balls of crust shuddered
        in the bush.

Birds will be
back as

though nothing has happened.
I am here to report that

nothing happened. Except
the oncologist said, then,
    benign.
    But now I hate

the moon. Hate the scar,
though it shines
    on her breast
    like the moon at my lips.

Too Many

my neighbors
say, when what they mean
      are deer—the foragers, the few at a time, fair

if little more
than rats, according to
      a farmer friend nearby, whose corn means plenty.

They nip the peaches,
and one bite ruins;
      hazard every road with their running-

into-headlights-
not-away; a
      menace; plague; something should be done.

   Or here in town,
where I've
      found a kind of afterlife—the townies hate

the damage to their varie-
gated hostas,
      shadeside ferns—what they do inside white bunkers of

the county's one good
course is "criminal,"
      deep scuffs through the sand—that's one thing—but

lush piles of polished-
olive-droppings, hoof-
        ruts in the chemically- and color-enriched greens . . .

    Yet here's
one more, curled
        like a tan seashell not a foot from my blade, just-

come-to-the-
world fawn, speckled,
        wet as a trout, which I didn't see, hacking back

brush beneath my tulip
poplar—it's not afraid,
        mews like a kitten, can't walk—there are so many, too

many of us,
the world keeps saying,
        and the world keeps making—this makes no sense—
            more.

Resurrection Man

1.
Let this body taketh
away sorrow.
      Let it asswageth furie of the mind
      with our hoard of bones.

—But she won't walk along
the path by my creek.
      Haunted, she hints,
      it's too muddy, it's steep,

let's go instead
to the woods. Let's look
      for mushrooms, let's divide bulbs, maybe
      the vultures are back in the beech trees, or

coltsfoot, yes,
maybe rue,
      maybe something's
      blooming or new. Let's build a footbridge over

the creek for
the dog. But
      not down there. The deer
      go down to die.

2.

    It's a hidden thicket fen

beside the creek
—hardly
    anything
    fits there or can pass—

where three springs
running I've
    stumbled over bones.
    A hoof, three skulls (one antlered), two

rib-structures
(intact), and many legs.
    I love the soup
    of it, primordial

ylem, for
the stuff from
    which the first elements
    formed. It's like that.

Moss stew, leaf-
pus, runoff,
    hidden stagnant
    mud and ripped-down sycamore skins and

cedar needles, ex-offal,
and who-knows-what-
      private-otherness where we step.
      Or not. How did

they know to come here?
For how long now?
      Driven out of dense woods
      by the new bright

Hummers, Beamers,
amped-
      up off-road
      dirt bikes . . .

3.
      I take the bones.

I fix them
in a sort of crèche
      in the barn. Resurrection
      man, after those who

supplemented incomes
by selling
      newly churchyard-unearthed
      bodies for dissection.

They simply
visited

those already
asleep eternally, sleep being
by its moisture, silence,
*and darkenes*s
our greatest calm.
That's how I feel

with the bones,
in the mud, where
foam grit gathers at the creek's
hard curve. She won't go there

but stands with me
staring at the PVC
drainpipes jutting from the hillside,
steady streams

lubricating the low deeryard.
What a sick,
I note, concoction.
Are you aware, she says—she just won't go—

4.
that means undigested
food? It's when
food-
fumes rise to the head

and the cold
brain congeals them.

Then, the body sleeps.
I know—at least—the bones. Hip socket like

a pickup coupling, rib
curved as
pheasant feather
and, after months in the mud, nearly as limber.

—But they have cut
the hills, sluiced the creek, flat-
tened out the soybean
fields, until it's all

(I mean three
hundred, for now,
acres) habitable
as a suburb. Which, I guess, it is,

such being
the social collateral
of progress, ingress, and the de-
naturing sprawl of the species.

Let this body taketh
away sorrow.
And yes—quickly, quickly
now, love—let's build a footbridge over

the creek. Soon we will all lie down, soon sleep.

NOTES

Posthumous Man. The passages about John Keats derive from several of his poems as well as his letter of July 25, 1819, to Fanny Brawne, and his famous last letter to Charles Brown, on November 30, 1820, in which he writes, "I have an habitual feeling of my real life having past, and that I am leading a posthumous existence."

Horse Madness. The detail about the eyes of goats and sheep comes from *At Day's Close: Night in Times Past* by A. Roger Ekirch. Other images and phrases derive from David Ferry's translation of *The Georgics of Virgil.*

On Overhearing. "The infinite is at hand only with respect to the finite" is from *The Writing of the Disaster* by Maurice Blanchot, translated by Ann Smock.

Ditches for the Poor. Some details in this poem come from Philippe Ariès's *Western Attitudes toward Death,* translated by Patricia M. Ranum. I found the passage by Emmanuel Levi-

nas in his *Otherwise Than Being: or Beyond Essence,* translated by
Alphonso Lingis.

1st My Children. During the Era of Manifestations, from 1837
to the late 1850s, a powerful religious revival swept through
American Shaker communities. According to the authors of
American Radiance (2001), thousands of gift messages and
songs were "received by inspiration" during this period, passed
along by "instruments" or Believers who articulated these spiri-
tual messages for fellow community members. Gift drawings
were one form of such messages. Polly Collins, from Berkshire
County, Massachusetts, was an active instrument whose gift
drawings are typified by distinctive squares or grids, inside of
which she often drew flowers, trees, and arbors. Above the grid
of trees I describe in my poem, Collins penned her own poem,
indicating each new stanza with a number.

Stranging. In 1528 Cabeza de Vaca traveled with a group of
Spanish explorers on the Narváez expedition to the New World,
landing near Tampa Bay, Florida. Eventually—one of only four
surviving members of the group—de Vaca made his way to
Mexico City, having explored widely in what is now Texas and
New Mexico. In 1537 he returned to Europe where he reported
his narrative to Charles V. De Vaca later sailed back to the New
World to serve as governor of Rio de la Plata in what is now
Paraguay and Argentina. His extensive report of experience
in the Americas appeared in 1555 as *Relación y Commentarios.* I
have used de Vaca's text and the translators' notes from *Álvar
Núñez Cabeza de Vaca: His Account, His Life, and the Expedition*

of Pánfilo de Narváez, edited and translated by Rolena Adorno and Patrick Charles Pautz.

My passage about the Puritan poet-minister Edward Taylor stems from several of his Preparatory Meditations, especially Meditation #77 from his Second Series, likely written in October of 1707. The poem's title comes from a passage in Taylor's "Gods Determinations": "Some gaze and Stare. Some stranging at the thing. . . . Some rage thereat."

Tis a Fayling. I have taken words, phrases, and information from the following sources: the editor's introduction and commentary to *The Poems of Michael Wigglesworth,* edited by Ronald A. Bosco; Michael Wigglesworth's jeremiad collection, *Meat Out of the Eater* (1670), a sequel to his best-selling work, *The Day of Doom* (1662); *The Diary of Michael Wigglesworth, 1653–1657: The Conscience of a Puritan,* edited by Edmund S. Morgan.

Middling. The machine described in the poem's third section is a "middling" mill for wheat grain. The whole grain is processed through a series of rotors and sifters that separate the grain's three elements—the hard outer husk, the "middling" or middle husk, and the inner soft material from which edible wheat flour is made.

One Willow. The Doctrine of Signatures is an expression of typology, holding that nature is a form of communication from the Deity; by careful observation of nature one can discern God's purposes. Paracelsus (born Phillip von Hohenheim), a Swiss physician (1493–1541), articulated the doctrine that was later picked up by Jakob Böhme in *De Signatura Rerum* (1621). Böhme described the medicinal uses of plants by deriving that use or purpose from some aspect of their form, name, or location of growth. Other proponents include William Coles (1626–1662), a botanist and author of *The Art of Simpling,* and Nicholas Culpeper, whose herbal manual (1653) paved the way to modern homeopathy. Recently Michel Foucault has used the Doctrine of Signatures in his theories of allegory and resemblance. A further application of the doctrine holds that nature provides a remedy for poisons or afflictions in the vicinity of those poisons; that's why, for instance, jewelweed grows beside poison ivy.

Bright Pitch. Simon Singh's *Big Bang: The Origin of the Universe* provided information on the development of nuclear weapons at the Manhattan Project, as well as details about "barns" or particle cross-sections.

Oriole. Some of the material comes from these sources: *Why Birds Sing: A Journey into the Mystery of Bird Song,* by David Rothenberg; *Field Guide to Birds of North America,* by Kenn Kaufman; *Birds of Ohio,* by Stan Tekiela; "Lemon Zest," by Jonathan Rosen, *The New York Times.* This poem is for Page.

Resurrection Man. Phrases in this poem's first stanza derive from William Vaughn's *Naturall and Artificial Directions for Health,* published in 1607. I took information about the illicit activities of "resurrection men" from *At Day's Close: Night in Times Past* by A. Roger Ekirch. In the early 1940s, physicist

George Gamow reinvigorated the word *ylem,* his name for the primal "hot soup" of neutrons, protons, and electrons produced by the Big Bang; *ylem* had been an obsolete Middle English term for the primordial substance from which the elements were formed.